rock
paper
scissors

SCENES FROM
a charmed divorce

Cathia Leonard Friou

SPARK Publications
Charlotte, North Carolina

Rock Paper Scissors: Scenes from a Charmed Divorce
Cathia Leonard Friou

Designed, produced, and published by SPARK Publications, SPARKpublications.com
Charlotte, NC
Cover Design and Illustration by Genna Hardgrove

BOOK OF AWAKENING © 2000 by Mark Nepo used with permission from Red Wheel Weiser, LLC, Newburyport, MA, www.redwheelweiser.com.
"The Layers" Copyright ©1978 by Stanley Kunitz, from THE COLLECTED POEMS by Stanley Kunitz. Used by permission of W. W. Norton & Company, Inc.
David Whyte quote printed with permission from Many Rivers Press, www.davidwhyte.com.

Printed in the United States of America.
Paperback, April 2018, ISBN: 978-1-943070-42-8
E-book, April 2018, ISBN: 978-1-943070-36-7

Family & Relationships / Divorce & Separation
Biography & Autobiography / Personal Memoirs
Family & Relationships / Life Stages / Mid-Life

I dedicate this book to
all who are walking the
unenviable path of divorce
and to the children they
are nurturing through it.

TABLE OF CONTENTS

PREFACE 9

Chapter 1   Late Summer 2001 11

Chapter 2   Spring 2009 19

Chapter 3   Spring 2010 23

Chapter 4   1984–2010 27

Chapter 5   December 1996 33

Chapter 6   Spring 2010 37

Chapter 7   2001–2008 43

Chapter 8   Spring 2011 49

Chapter 9   Fall 2011 53

Chapter 10   Winter 2011 57

Chapter 11   Spring 2011 .... **63**

Chapter 12   Summer 2012.. **69**

Chapter 13   Summer 2012.. **77**

Chapter 14   Summer 2012.. **83**

Chapter 15   Summer 2012.. **89**

Chapter 16   Fall 2015.. **93**

Chapter 17   Spring 2014 .... **99**

Chapter 18   2010–2015 .... **107**

Chapter 19   Summer 2014.. **111**

Chapter 20   2006–2015 .... **117**

Chapter 21   Summer 2017.. **123**

Chapter 22   Summer 2017.. **127**

Chapter 23   Late Summer 2017....................................... **131**

ACKNOWLEDGMENTS **137**

To journey without being changed
is to be a nomad.
To change without journeying
is to be a chameleon.
To journey and to be transformed
by the journey
is to be a pilgrim.

– MARK NEPO

PREFACE

Our story could never be a country music song.

We didn't leave each other for another. We didn't have to sell the family home. I didn't have to go back to work to support myself. There wasn't addiction, domestic violence, or mental illness in the mix. We didn't have to split friends or jockey for alliances. Our children continue to thrive.

I've learned that divorce is an illusion, especially when kids are involved. You can end the marriage, live apart, date other people, even fall in love again, and you are still tied to the other person in ways you may not realize and almost certainly don't want.

While married, I came to believe that marriage is a flawed institution, and now I see that divorce is too.

Originally, this was going to be a book about my adventures walking the Camino de Santiago, but that's not the book that wanted to be written. Instead, it's about my inner odyssey on the path of divorce—the metaphorical Camino I've been walking since 2010.

The author Dani Shapiro says that writing a memoir is "not about what happened, but what the *fuck* happened."

How do you walk away from a highly functional relationship and a perfectly good guy? How do you pledge fidelity to your soul and agree to blow up your life simultaneously? How do you jerk the rug out from under your children and assign yourself sole accountability for changing the trajectory of their ten- and twelve-year-old lives?

When was the first time we did or said something or left something unsaid that put us on the path to divorce? If a warning bell had sounded, could we have righted ourselves? Or does marriage have a shelf life and our time was simply up?

Was it all just a big misunderstanding, the uncoupling? Did I make it all up? Could we have tried harder, different, better? If we're this civil and even friendly, then why, exactly, did we split up?

This is the story of a charmed divorce.

CHAPTER 1
LATE SUMMER 2001

When our four-year-old daughter, Julia, learns we're moving to New York City for her father's new job she squeals, "Thanks, Daddy! That's where Cinderella lives!"

My designer friend tells me to paint the entire apartment "Nantucket Gray." One of Benjamin Moore's historical colors, it feels like a great way out of the dreaded apartment-beige that came with the place. A corner unit on the twenty-ninth floor, the utilitarian two-bedroom has sweeping views of the East River and the Triborough Bridge and a much-coveted kitchen window. Largely charm-free with the ubiquitous parquet floors, it isn't nearly as lovely as the home we're leaving behind, but no one is more eager than I am to ditch life-as-we-know-it in Charlotte.

My husband, Stuart, and I spend a few days moving into our apartment. I'm impressed with the amount of natural light and the impact of the paint. More olive-green and not one bit gray, it's a substantial color. All the furniture we brought fits perfectly, and while it feels like a dollhouse or a movie set, it smells like possibility, and I'm ecstatic to be an official Manhattanite.

While we settle in, our children are still in Charlotte with my parents. Julia and her almost-two-year-old sister, Claire, are barely aware of the new lifestyle we're jumping into, but my parents are crestfallen to be losing their grandchildren to New York City.

When we swing open the doors and welcome the girls home a few days later, they are tickled to see their new, shared bedroom that now doubles as a playroom. Twin beds with white quilts and plaid bed skirts flank the wall with the covered radiator. The sunny room has a large picture window that slides open only six inches. At the foot of the bed with a retractable guardrail sits the tiny TV that operates as a display for their extensive collection of Disney VHS tapes.

Much to their surprise, the "Moving Fairy" has delivered Polly Pocket dolls welcoming them to their new house. Giddy with the excitement of the day, they never once ask where the upstairs is or how to get to the backyard. With novelties like a trash chute down the hall and a communal rooftop with chaise lounges and trees in giant planters, the new digs seem to suit the girls just fine.

We have a few weeks before preschool begins, and we traipse around town like the tourists we are, hoping time and familiarity will turn us into locals. We head out with Claire strapped into her fancy Maclaren stroller, the one my knowledgeable city friend said we just had to have. Julia walks beside us, often holding onto the arm of the stroller and needing lots of breaks as her young legs get used to walking the streets. We later learn about a skateboard-type attachment for the stroller that allows her to hitch a ride anytime she's tired.

Our very first family outing is to nearby Carl Schurz Park that runs along the East River's esplanade. A mini Central Park designed by the same architect, this secret garden is not likely to be found on any New York City must-see list. There is an elaborate playground at the south end of the park with a series of bright red play stations, a set of swings that fly high enough to make *my* stomach leap, and a rudimentary water feature in the middle of a vast cement box with four-inch walls. The playground is alive with littles of all ages, most of them under the charge of a nanny.

After leaving the park, we drop into a bodega for a quick snack before heading home. Out front, arrays of fresh-cut flowers burst from plastic paint buckets. These mom-and-pop convenience stores pepper the neighborhood, fixtures in our new urban lifestyle. Another few blocks and we're back in our lobby, the girls fighting over who gets to push the elevator buttons to take us home.

The morning the towers fall, the girls and I are in the apartment. It should have been the first day of preschool for Claire, but she is home with a cold. I'm irritated. *Who's sick on the first day of school?* Julia doesn't start for another few days, and the girls are happily playing together in their room. The phone rings while I'm unloading the dishwasher.

"Do you know what's happening in your city right now?" asks my friend Robert.

"Charlotte? What's happening in Charlotte?" I say, assuming he means my hometown.

Immediately I switch on the television and learn a plane has crashed into the World Trade Center. Within moments

I hear Robert's officemates gasp in the background as we all witness the second plane strike.

Official Manhattanites for just three weeks, I have no idea what to do or what to think. Making sure the girls are content and fully distracted, I move from the family room to the master, so I can watch the news coverage in private. The small bedroom TV rests high on a dresser and faces away from the door. Stuart calls to say he doesn't think the girls and I should leave the apartment, adding he doesn't know what time he'll be leaving the office. I can't imagine what he plans to do with the stock market closed for the day and can't understand why he doesn't want to hunker down at home with us, but I don't fight him about it.

His suggestion that we stay put leaves me feeling even more uneasy. This is a man whom I jokingly refer to as "Safety Sam." He's not a door locker unless he's leaving town and often tosses his car keys on the floor mat of his Jeep. Not one to catastrophize, even during a catastrophe, it takes a lot to rattle him.

Stay at home today?

If this were the late '80s, he'd be working away on the ninety-second floor of the North Tower in his first post-college job. Now he has an office in Midtown, so he isn't part of the disaster area and finally makes it home midafternoon. Somehow the buses are still operating, and his two-mile commute home is uneventful. Subways are long since halted, and yellow cabs are fleeing the island, with or without patrons. The normally congested FDR Drive that we can see out our window is barren. The city is on lockdown.

The days following are eerily quiet and somber. The parks are suddenly full of fathers, and missing-person flyers line the windows and doors of local merchants. Haze from the smoldering pile eventually makes its way to our neighborhood, a reminder of the horror downtown.

We keep our date night a few nights later and drink beer at Dorian's on Second Avenue. We sit at an uneven table covered with a plastic-coated, red-checkered tablecloth. We're there with other neighbors, all strangers yet now intimately connected, ingesting the same news coverage we've been watching nonstop since Tuesday on the multiple screens throughout the bar. It doesn't feel particularly good to be out, and we head home sooner than planned.

The stock market, which is my husband's motherboard, doesn't reopen until the following week. It's the longest market shutdown since 1933. Improbably, none of this delays the opening of his new investment firm a few weeks later.

It will be years before our girls know what happened that day. While my enchantment with the city is waning before the planes leave the runway that fateful September morning, it's several months before the shiny starts to wear off for Julia. "I like Charlotte more better than New York," she tells me one day lying on the couch together.

"Oh, Tootsie, I understand. City life can be hard sometimes, but we're on a great adventure together!" I say to her in my upbeat voice. I so want to believe this.

I feed my mind this narrative every day, like an IV drip, but my heart is having none of it. I'm already planning our escape.

The truth is rarely pure
and never simple.

– OSCAR WILDE

CHAPTER 2
SPRING 2009

I've heard that a woman knows her marriage is over about a year before it actually ends. It's Kentucky Derby weekend when I come to understand my marriage is ending.

I'm not in Louisville for what is supposed to be my first Derby experience with a whole host of friends and festivities. Instead, I'm attending the funeral of a dear friend's mother. Stuart is traveling on to the Derby without me, and I find great relief in being left behind.

I don't know how the divorce will play out exactly, but I know in my bones we're done. Mine That Bird wins the 135th Run for the Roses in a monumental upset, and by the time the same jockey wins on a different horse the following year, Stuart and I are announcing our separation.

There is no trigger event to our uncoupling, just a gradual bloodletting of the life force. Provider par excellence, he doesn't beat me, cheat on me, or mistreat me in any way. It's a glacially slow growing apart—"death by a thousand paper cuts" as I often describe it.

Ironically, it's a phrase I'd picked up long ago from my financier husband referencing a portfolio of stocks, each down a little and collectively representing a big loss.

And the day came
when the risk to remain
tight in a bud was
more painful than the
risk it took to blossom.

– ANAÏS NIN

CHAPTER 3
SPRING 2010

Sitting on a bench in a park near our house, we try to make sense of what's happening in our lives. High-school sweethearts married for eighteen years, we are trying to digest the dismantling of our lives. And it seems we have no better tools in our forties than when we met as teenagers.

Gasping for the last bits of marital air, the cabin pressure dropping precipitously, I ask him a question.

"Do you think I ask too much of marriage?"

In a single, exhausted exhale he replies, "For someone like you, no. But what you ask of me, yes."

And there it is. All the years of confusion and underlying pain, the months and months of marriage counseling, no one could pinpoint it as precisely as the man living it.

It's a story I tell people often both for its economy of words, one of his specialties, and its piercing truth. I believe it's the beginning of a kind of belated intimacy. He validates my hunger, and I get a glimpse into the pain I'm causing him in longing for something more.

How shall the heart be reconciled
to its feast of losses?

– STANLEY KUNITZ

CHAPTER 4
1984–2010

We marry several times over our twenty-six years together.

The first time is in high school, shortly after we meet. At a school carnival, you can marry your honey for a dollar, replete with faux ring, veil, and a makeshift tux for the lucky groom. In the photo, I'm wearing striped leggings, and he has on a Key Club t-shirt and plastic top hat.

The second time we marry, it is in the full and traditional sense. It is exactly eight years after our first date. Many breakups, other relationships, and reconciliations pepper the years, but on an unseasonably warm day in February (one of the slowest sports months, per the groom's request), I walk down the aisle of Christ Episcopal Church. My brocade, off-the-shoulder dress with plenty of pleats helps shield the nervous shake of my right leg as we exchange vows that afternoon.

The third time we marry is a few years later in Las Vegas. An idea that starts with the thrill of spying a drive-through wedding chapel ends anticlimactically with a renewal of vows when we learn it is illegal to marry someone you are already married to. After only a few words, the female chaplain with spiked red hair and a toothy grin leans out the window to give us our certificate of renewal as if it is a burger and fries.

Eighteen years to the month of our official "I do," I tell him I don't want to anymore. I am just home from a solo, soul-searching trip—a getaway to Arizona planned specifically to unpack my marriage and wager blowing up my life. In front of the fireplace, I tell him I want a divorce. Sunlight is beaming through the French doors, and the children are playing in the neighborhood. It is a hushed and brief conversation ending with him saying to me, "I hope the grass will be greener for you."

As we are nearing the end of marriage counseling that morphed into intentional divorce counseling (in other words, how-to-do-this-to-our-kids counseling), it happens. One afternoon I step out of our therapist's office for a quick trip to the restroom, catching my wedding ring on the door handle. The platinum bends into my finger, and I quickly shimmy out of the ring before my finger has a chance to swell.

I take it as a sign that the marriage is over and a good omen that we are on the right track. There had been so many signs before, from the symbol of all the lights burning out simultaneously in our house to the chilling dream I had about us driving a horse and buggy dragging the corpses of a bride and groom behind us. And on what was to be our last family vacation together, over Easter, we were riding bikes in Key West early one morning while the kids were still in the hotel room. We ended up on a dead-end street surrounded by an ancient cemetery.

Both ominous and soothing, death and decay are everywhere I turn. It will occur to my future self that I could just as easily interpret the message of the bent ring as, "Stay put, child." But I sense my soul is dying on the vine, and I have to stay on course.

One does not discover new lands
without consenting to lose sight
of the shore for a very long time.

– ANDRÉ GIDE

CHAPTER 5
DECEMBER 1996

I'm about nine weeks pregnant, and I start to feel a twinge in my ovaries. I can't identify the feeling exactly, but a great sense of despair begins to envelop me. We're at the ten-year reunion of Stuart's fraternity pledge class in some forgettable hotel off of I-85, and I'm the only one in the room who isn't drinking. I tell him I'm scared, that I want to go lie down. He's frustrated but walks me back to the room because it's the right thing to do.

I cry and try to convey how much pressure it is to carry a baby when your body only knows how to lose them—how lying down instead of standing up gives me an absurd sense of control to keep that baby up in there where it belongs. He nods and tells me everything will be okay, reminding me of the favorable ultrasound a few weeks ago.

It's all in my head, of course, but that's what two miscarriages have done to me. I don't feel one bit secure or even capable, but like an inadequate waif. I didn't weigh enough in high school to give blood. What if I'm not hardy enough to bring a live baby into the world? The lost pregnancies, less than six months apart, were my first brushes with grief and mourning.

While he sits on the bed with me and tries to show compassion, the noise of his frat brothers down below proves too compelling. He tells me to rest and promises he won't be long. We both know it's not true.

After he leaves, I prop my feet up higher and pray with all my might that I won't leave a third baby in the toilet tonight.

There are some things you learn
best in calm, and some in storm.

– WILLA CATHER

CHAPTER 6
SPRING 2010

The marriage therapist suggests we continue living together for ten days after announcing our separation to the children. Because they're accustomed to their father being out of town several nights a week for several years now, the idea is to create security and continuity in the wake of the news. This seems reasonable to both of us, and why not? We've been living civil but parallel lives for over a year, so what's another week and a half under the same roof?

I'm a big fan of our therapist, even though he doesn't save our marriage. He's an older man who wears a gold chain and full beard. He came highly recommended from a friend, and I liked him immediately. He has mismatched but comfortable furniture in his roomy office and occasionally uses a whiteboard with us to teach new concepts. He cracks corny jokes and sometimes sighs through pursed lips. He feels both father figure and peer to me.

Drinking wine on the back porch on night seven, Stuart and I talk separation logistics instead of catching up on the week or trading tales from the *New York Times* like we used to. We're sitting in our favorite chairs, my legs curled beneath me, scheming about how to furnish on the cheap. Having moved twelve times in eighteen years of marriage, I'm a whiz kid at setting up new homes, and now there's the business of establishing his-and-her satellite locations.

We tell the kids they won't have to shuttle back and forth, that Mommy and Daddy will be the ones to come and go. Thinking myself awfully resourceful and a smidge clever when I hatch this plan, I later learn I didn't invent this thing called "nesting," where the baby birds stay put while the mama bird and daddy bird fly in and out of the nest. As with most of my ideas, Stuart goes along agreeably.

Initially, I assume we'll share a single apartment, but he's immediately resistant, and I'm confused. Given his pragmatism and frugality, I'm surprised he insists we both need our own places. "I'm not coming home to your Oprah magazines on the coffee table," he says. Hmm, I'd never heard him complain about that before. I guess he wants the place to exude bachelor pad and not clearly-a-woman-lives-here-too vibes. Fair enough.

He chooses a rental house that has a bird's-eye view of a house we used to share and where we welcomed our second child. His new place is a modest house with high ceilings and a front porch, and puts him back in his favorite neighborhood. I imagine he's thrilled to be returning to his old jogging route as well.

One afternoon we meet at his new house, so I can see the space and measure the rooms as I've offered to set up his house for him. Standing in the empty living room together, he introduces me to the realtor. "This is my friend, Cathia."

Friend? We've been married for almost two decades and doing life together much longer, friend. I lost my virginity to you, friend. I bore you two daughters, friend. Friend?

I'll move him twice more, post-divorce, all in the name of creating a warm and inviting home for our girls. And to prove we are not a fractured family, merely a reorganized one. And because I'm really good at it and enjoy doing it. And because this is my contribution.

The dog is lying at my feet as our night-seven porch conversation continues. I tell Stuart I'll order the new beds the following day and confirm he wants a queen like I'm getting for myself. I say it like I'm confirming his order for sushi takeout. Dismantling life as we know it and simultaneously carving out our new normal seem to cancel each other out. I'm neither pained nor excited, just energetically getting the job done.

"Do you resent having to give me half the money?" I ask.

"Not really. I'm glad I'm able to set your ass up."

I feel relief. I'm both grateful for North Carolina law that dictates splitting marital assets in half and also mildly guilty that I haven't financially contributed to our household income since the early '90s. Yet, I've been the primary caregiver and house manager, and there was never any expectation for me to work outside the home.

The invisible mist of *his money* will follow me for the next seven years.

Noticing our drinks are getting low, we fall into the old habit of choosing who has to get up—to answer the doorbell, fetch the crying baby, refill the drinks. Without hesitation, we begin our well-worn practice of the game Rock Paper Scissors. After we both throw the same hand three times, he beats me on the fourth throw, his rock crushing my scissors.

As I step inside to refill our glasses, he gently calls out to me, "How can you say we aren't still connected?"

All the research, planning, and anticipation can't shield me from the absolute shattering I feel as Stuart leaves the house for the final time. As status quo as each of the last ten days feels, he doesn't kiss me goodbye or whisper "I love you" as he heads out to catch an early morning flight that last day. I'm pretending to still be asleep as I hear the front door close, and in that moment, it's as if a priceless piece of pottery has slipped from the mantel and crashed to the floor.

Life is a creative,
intimate, and unpredictable
conversation.

– DAVID WHYTE

CHAPTER 7
2001–2008

New York City is the crack pipe I smoke when bored. I live there twice and seriously consider a third move. Still, I'm not sure why the place has such a hold on me.

After my first urban experiment goes awry, I decide the suburbs of New York are the answer. But wouldn't you know, Westchester County doesn't suit me either (though I love having my car back and a yard for the girls). Sadly, the suburban serenity feels stifling, and the city feels much further away than the forty-minute train ride.

So not long after our move to the 'burbs, I tell Stuart I want to move the family back to Charlotte and have him commute to his job each week. Deftly, I plead my case. "We never see you anyway. You leave before the girls wake up and are home after they go to bed. So what's the difference?"

He isn't keen on the idea, but he is eager for a happy wife, so he agrees.

He never once complains about getting on an airplane to New York every Monday morning and flying back home to

Charlotte every Thursday night. An hour-and-fifteen-minute flight means a three-hour, door-to-door commute when all goes well, which it miraculously almost always does.

We live like this for four years until one day I decide I want another go at living in the Big Apple. He agrees, and with little hesitation, we pack everything up. We have a big yard sale (again), put a few things in storage (again), and head back to the city.

"Your husband must be over the moon you are all back in the city under one roof," gushes my new friend Jane. Given that I've scarcely seen him "over the moon" about anything other than perhaps a Tar Heels win or a big day in the market, her comment short-circuits my brain. I smile and say, "Yes, of course," and change the topic to something mundane.

Her comment sits on my chest for weeks. *Surely he's glad we are all back together and he's no longer commuting each week. Surely he notices the difference and feels relief. Surely he thinks this is better than before.*

I'm full of energy tackling the city a second time because this time I'm a professional Manhattanite. I know all the things I need to dwell well there, and we've solved for them all. We have a car in the city, a washer/dryer inside our apartment, and the girls are enrolled in a dream of a school to carry them until graduation (if we chose to stay that long). It's a well-curated recipe to set us up for success this time.

I realize I've made a mistake almost as quickly as the first go-round. Before I can get my confession out of my mouth, Stuart tries to stop me. Shaking his head, holding up his hand like a white-gloved traffic cop, he tries to keep me from saying what he knows is about to tumble out of my mouth.

My enchantment with New York City appears to last approximately two weeks. I finally discover that I enjoy moving to the city far more than actually living there. And at the end of the school year, we pack up and head back home to Charlotte. It is my idea (again), and he goes along with it (again).

Not all those who wander are lost.

– J. R. R. TOLKIEN

CHAPTER 8
SPRING 2011

Our goal is to nest until the last bird goes to college—a seven-year arc.

We make it one year.

I think it is the grocery list that kills it. Etched into the thick pad on the pantry wall in his unmistakable handwriting is the word "Coke." Uncharitably, I read it as, "I'll need more Cokes for my twice-monthly visit to the children in the house I paid for." Of course, he means no such thing, but I'm nearing the end of my enchantment with our decision to nest.

Inexplicably I feel homeless, though I have a very comfortable apartment nearby, a nest of my own every other weekend. It is perfectly lovely—and also vacant of any life. No kids, no animals, no regular comings and goings. The furnishings are bright and well appointed, but the energy is heavy. And there is no hiding the grief that follows me there and sleeps in that bed with me each night.

The guys we hire to move Stuart into his own place plunk down all of his furniture in the driveway instead of loading the individual pieces onto the truck as they come out of the house. It's disquieting to see all our stuff, things we'd divvied up with ease, sitting on display for all to see and speculate about. It could pass for a garage sale or what I imagine a court-ordered eviction might look like.

A few weeks later, I paint the trim in his former home office robin's-egg blue and buy all new furniture. I name it my "1940s Hollywood Den," and it resembles an elegant, boutique-hotel lobby. While I pass through it routinely, I can't say I ever use it.

I eventually decide to downsize. I've never loved the house, and it feels particularly mammoth when the girls are with Stuart. I sell it two years later to a cute young family with a full-price offer and buy something half the size in our old neighborhood—the same neighborhood where Stuart has been living since the day we split.

Never confuse movement
with action.

– ERNEST HEMINGWAY

CHAPTER 9
FALL 2011

I spy an explosion of color through the beveled glass windows of the double front door. On the pristine brick floor of the covered stoop in a heap of paisley and swirl, four different Vera Bradley tote bags wait for me to bring them inside.

Every other Monday, after he takes our kids to school, Stuart drops their bags on the front porch of our once-shared house. Somehow I never see him when he pulls in the driveway, but when I stumble upon the view of the bags, it always startles me. This evidence of the sterile kid exchange now that we no longer "nest" feels out of step with who we are trying to be as a family.

Life is not a problem
to be solved, but a reality
to be experienced.

– SØREN KIERKEGAARD

CHAPTER 10
WINTER 2011

I sign up for Match.com at the absolute insistence of my friend Jennifer. Divorced for three years, she knows a little something about how hard it is to meet people when all your friends are married. Separated for eight months, I am eager to date. However, the thought of going online feels so ... how shall I put it? Desperate, pathetic, ever-so-slightly seedy, and did I mention desperate?

I fight her at every turn. Her examples of positive encounters and even relationships that materialized are met with a "yeah, but ..." from me. Even knowing a friend who recently married a guy she met on Match, I am resistant.

She bugs me until I finally give in and sign up. Finding a few tasteful photos of myself and none that include my children, I write my profile and activate my account.

In completing the profile, I make it amply clear who I am by checking certain boxes that give information about political and religious beliefs, among other things. Trust me when I tell you that in reading my profile it is clear that I am (a) liberal, (b) spiritual but not religious, and (c) done having kids.

So you can imagine my confusion when, for example, someone comments that he is eager to meet a fertile woman or when an über-conservative expresses exceptional interest in me. *Are these men actually reading my profile or just flipping through the pictures?*

I find it best to get to the coffee date (or glass of wine) as soon as possible. It makes no sense in my mind to build a bunch of virtual rapport only to learn that the 3D version of the person doesn't match up with what I've cooked up in my head.

My mantra: it's all crap until you meet someone in person.

I gather many entertaining emails along the way, but the best of all comes from an older admirer in Myrtle Beach, South Carolina. It can only be placed in the "you can't make this shit up" category and is an utterly priceless relic from my (initial) twelve days on Match:

> WOW...Pretty Lady...You Got My Attention!!!
> This is ▓▓▓▓▓ in Myrtle Beach. Thoroughly
> enjoyed reading your Bio...and do hope you
> will take a moment to read mine.
>
> Must confess that I am extremely
> impressed...LOVELY PICTURES and a
> CLASSY LADY. Very few Ladies have been
> blessed to Command Attention...but you
> certainly have that Rare Quality. You appear
> to be an Exceptional W.O.M.A.N.....and I
> defiantly want to know your entire story.

For what ever reason "Your Pictures" remind me of another Beautiful Lady and my most favorite film. The stunning Vivien Leigh, along with Clark Gable.. in "Gone With The Wind"...what a great flick!!

The part that "Your Pictures" bring to my mind and imagination... is when: Rhett Butler tells Scarlett O'Hara.. "You need to be Kissed Hard and Often.by Someone that Knows How". My further comment to You would be..."My Dear it would certainly be My Pleasure and an Honor". Unfortunately Scarlett was a totally confused bitch....and blew it big time. But it's only a movie.

So please read my bio and see if you think We could finish the Rhett and Scarlett story??Don't make the same mistake that Scarlett did...I hear she's still picking cotton in Atlanta.

Not exactly sure how Rhett Butler would have written this letter to you...but I'll give it my best shot. So as a Southern Gentleman...a Man of Honor and Integrity...and Someone quite "Taken with You", I humbly request that you allow me the courtesy and privilege to come Court and Pursue you. For I now feel ever so strongly that "You need to be Kissed Hard and Often by this Worthy Gentleman".

My journey to you can be quite swift as I Anxiously Await to be in the presence of your Lovely company. My Dear with tremendous Anticipation and Excitement...I await your decision. *****Remember Scarlett's famous Blunder and where it got her: ****"I can't think about that right now...if I do I'll go crazy...I'll think about that tomorrow".

Sincerely looking forward to hearing back from you soon.

I merely took the
energy it takes to pout
and wrote some blues.

– DUKE ELLINGTON

CHAPTER 11
SPRING 2011

One of the lighter scenes in the off-Broadway show *The Last Five Years* is the hilarious song *Shiksa Goddess*. Jamie is gaga at having met Cathy, a remarkable woman who isn't Jewish like he is. He sings about all the things she could be that wouldn't matter to him—tattooed, bald, pierced, criminal—just as long as she isn't Jewish.

A shiksa myself—though I can't confirm the goddess part—it is bittersweet to hum along to the catchy tune as I reflect on having said goodbye to a wonderfully intriguing Jewish man who had captured my heart.

We meet on Match.com, and our first date is a long conversation over coffee and tea peppered with cerebral sparring on a wide range of topics: personality assessments, politics, and poetry. Flying from one thought-provoking subject to the next, we cover a lot of ground in those two hours.

"I could *never* fall in love with you," he tells me at one point on the date. "You have the same Myers-Briggs typology as my ex-wife."

The hubris is stunning and also mildly attractive. I feel compelled to prove I am more than my score on a personality assessment and that he can't possibly know whether or not we'll fall in love. His comment plus his general disposition proves irresistible to me. "Like catnip," muses my friend Katie.

I'm new to post-divorce dating and am impressed with my luck in matching with this guy. While the second-best outcome of a first date is mutual disappointment, the very *best* possible outcome of a first date is intrigue. Check plus here!

We date for several months, his conflicted state riding shotgun in our relationship from the early days. Intoxicated by each other and new love, it is easy to ignore at first. Teetering between having found "the perfect woman but for her faith"—his words—and being completely unable to introduce me to his rabbi and confidant, his cognitive dissonance is getting the better of us.

Once I fully understand his long-term plan to begin living an Orthodox life with an Orthodox wife, I realize there is an insurmountable disconnect. Confronting him about the absurdity of me being a part of that picture, he tells me that because I am such an open-minded person he thought I would be open to the idea of converting and living the life of an Orthodox Jewish woman.

What?! Where on God's green Earth could he have possibly gotten that idea? Has he met me?

He is genuinely stunned to learn I have no vision or appetite for the possibility of it.

I'm stunned myself and start to feel somewhat hoodwinked by the whole relationship. With a deep yearning to grow in his faith, he keeps a kosher kitchen but not a kosher bedroom.

I tell him to quit dating non-Jewish women as a first step and to start following his path in earnest. I also tell him that if he has to choose between God and me, by all means choose God. I make it abundantly clear that I don't think God cares what kind of blood courses through my veins, but that since he does, he needs to change his behavior. I'm having to life coach my boyfriend into breaking up with me, and I am beginning to resent it.

When I finally own that I am like chili cheese fries to a man on a diet, I break it off with him, even though it's he who should step away from the table. And when I later learn he is living his Orthodox life with his Orthodox wife, I am both gutted and perversely complimented.

The cut worm forgives the plow.

– WILLIAM BLAKE

CHAPTER 12
SUMMER 2012

Watching the movie *The Way* sparks something in me. It is set along the Camino de Santiago (in English, the Way of Saint James), a pilgrimage route across northern Spain. By the time the credits roll, I say out loud to no one in particular, "I want to do that."

I decide to walk the second half of the Camino, and a few months later I fly to Madrid, take a train to León, and walk 200 miles to Santiago de Compostela over a two-week period. My friends joke that it sounds like my *Eat, Pray, Love* tour.

I don't walk the Camino to mourn or make sense of the loss of my eighteen-year marriage. My grief journey has been plenty robust so far, and I'm not running low on professional analysis or personal rumination.

I've been seeing a therapist off and on for several years. The years of Jungian analysis didn't salvage or erode my marriage, nor was it designed to, but it did put me in deeper touch with the reality that I was intensely lonely inside my marriage and could no longer subsist on crumbs.

On my third day walking, I embark on a slow and steady climb to the village of Rabanal. I walk alone the entire day. The tan and dusty path that leads out of town is narrow at points but offers expansive views all around. I pass many of my fellow pilgrims on my way up the modest incline with several making note of my speedy pace. I am totally unaware of the number of people I am passing until the third or fourth comment.

I am attacking the path and for what? There is no rush to get to the next village, no personal best time I am trying to beat. I am in the middle of Spain, two years out of my marriage, having the adventure of a lifetime, and somehow squandering it with my rapid pace.

And then it starts—with the faint sound of cowbells as backdrop.

I begin talking to the Camino as if it is my former husband. Not out loud, but a very real conversation—diatribe, actually—is ensuing. At some point, this one-way conversation with the path morphs into a rant directed at Stuart, and it goes a little something like this:

> *I know we've been apart for more than two years and are now officially divorced, but enough already. When I get home, we are getting back together. To hell with your current relationship and any other life plans you might have in the hopper. And to hell with how you feel about me or us … you're coming with me.*
>
> *We've learned a lot over the last few years, and the main thing I've learned is that we need to be married again. I totally understand how it fell apart, but what I know now is that it*

wasn't designed to be a permanent condition.
Enough is enough.

Obviously, I wasn't clear enough with you the
two times I broached the topic of reconciliation
before. I let you shut it down before it even got
off the ground—and shame on me—but that
was then, and this is now, buddy. And we aren't
merely exploring anymore; we're doing this
thing. And for keeps this time.

We'll have to remarry, of course, but it's just
paperwork, right? I've tackled harder things, and
I can't be bothered with logistics right now. I have
a once-in-a-lifetime trip I need to get back to.

A great exhale (or was it a harrumph?) marks the end of
my ranting. The mild anxiety is now at bay because I have
a plan. Now I can enjoy my trip and fully immerse in the
culture, all the while convinced I can make things right with
Stuart upon my return.

For the first year or so of the separation, I was in a lot
of pain and actively grieving, but it never felt wrong. But
lately something feels deeply, horribly wrong with the whole
divorce enterprise.

About six months before I walked the Camino, I wrote
a lengthy email outlining ten or so speculations as to why
the separation suddenly felt wrong and why I wanted to

talk about the possibility of reconciliation. I'm not sure reconciliation is viable, but I know that something is tugging at my gut on a regular basis, and I can no longer leave all of this unsaid. And since divorce papers are in the works at the time, the clock was literally ticking.

Part of the email reads as follows:

> *I don't know if it is denial or intuition or some funky holding pattern on the non-linear grief track, but somehow I harbor hope for us.*
>
> *Maybe it's merely the last gasp of grief for me knowing the divorce will be final next month.*
>
> *Maybe it's because you are at an empty-canvas place in life, and I want desperately to share that with you.*
>
> *Maybe it's because I know you are hurting, and I want to comfort you.*
>
> *Maybe it's because I believe we could do life together differently now that we've been apart for so long and learned so much in nineteen months.*
>
> *Maybe it's because you are in a relationship, and I'm currently not.*
>
> *Maybe it's because of all the research I've done this fall on divorce and co-parenting.*
>
> *Maybe it's because I no longer find marriage the flawed institution, but divorce.*

Rock Paper Scissors

Maybe it's because a true and full break is all we ever really needed.

Maybe it's because I can't imagine spending the rest of our lives apart knowing we still have love for one another.

Maybe it's all of these things and more.

He responded kindly enough but with a clear lack of seeing my vision. He told me it was difficult for him to imagine a scenario where we could happily reconcile and that all the same issues would still be there. He said he both loved and resented me, reminding me that the marriage counselor and I had both said that just because two people love each other doesn't mean they should be married.

Ouch.

That should have been the end of the discussion, especially since we submitted the paperwork to make the divorce final a few weeks later. But here I am six months later and 3,500 miles from home hatching a master plan to remarry my ex-husband.

It isn't enough for me to have largely orchestrated the divorce; I am now going to solely orchestrate the reconciliation. That he has a girlfriend of a year at this point is of no consequence to me whatsoever. *He's mine and I want him back*, the two-year-old inside me cries. *That marriage had to die, yes, but we* belong *together. We can create a new and better marriage.*

I miss him, or maybe it is the container of marriage and family that I miss. I miss the familiar, the calm, the predictable. And what relief washes over me as I concoct my tidy-box plan, something I later coin the "Reclamation Project." Deeply satisfied, I feel fully present and anchored and sense the Earth is suddenly back on its right axis. I proceed to walk the rest of the day's thirteen-mile journey completely liberated.

By the following evening, I am under the spell of Mr. Tall, Dark & Handsome, and all bets are off.

When the soul wishes to
experience something she
throws an image of the
experience out before her and
enters into her own image.

– MEISTER ECKHART

CHAPTER 13
SUMMER 2012

I know right away he is not a pilgrim like the rest of us. His shoes are a dead giveaway. Unlike the bloodied and bandaged feet peering out of flip flops and man sandals, he sports shiny leather loafers protecting perfectly tanned feet. In white linen shorts, Mr. Tall, Dark & Handsome charmingly inserts himself into our conversation. Well after 10 p.m., the sun has only recently set as he joins us for a glass of red wine at Casa Marcos.

It's my fourth day of walking the Camino as I cross a bridge to enter the village of Molinaseca. I chat with some fellow pilgrims and then walk down the main street looking for my hotel. Already self-conscious about staying in hotels when the norm is to stay in hostels, or *albergues* as they're called, I'm embarrassed by Hotel de Floriana. Most of the hotels along the Camino are varying degrees of modest inns, but this one sticks out in its loveliness. Newer and larger, replete with my own hair dryer in the room (what luxury!), I feel particularly indulgent this night.

After I check in, I head out to the courtyard to journal. "I'm not sure when I've been so content," I write on that early evening in late June as tunes from the '70s waft in the background. *California Dreaming* is pouring from hidden speakers, and I'm writing about being tired after walking sixteen miles but pushing through to meet up with fellow pilgrims for drinks and dinner. The sun is still shining brightly, and it's the seven rings of the church bells that alert me to close my yellow Moleskine notebook and ready up for the evening.

Once I shower I meet back up with friends at Casa Marcos. My twenty-something, Irish friend Rebecca and I recount the day's path and how the weather has been so mercurial—wind and cold, sun and clouds, putting sweatshirt on, taking sweatshirt off. While we're sitting at a red plastic table along the main cobblestone path through town, an entirely new creature joins us.

A native New Yorker, we learn, he is strikingly handsome, statuesque, and sporting an impressive head of hair. Fluent in the language and customs of Spain, it doesn't take long for this girl to fall under his spell. The group conversation continues, and then Rebecca leaves to go back to her hostel for the night.

Realizing we are staying in the same hotel, he invites me to join him for a nightcap in the lobby. I have an eighteen-mile hike ahead of me the next morning. I agree to one glass.

We talk for hours. More accurately, I listen for hours with an occasional contribution. And for the extreme extrovert I am and on the journey of a lifetime, I'm rather surprised at my quiet self. Then again, I'm not sure I've known such a large personality. Many years in the intelligence community and deeply tied to 9/11, this is no ordinary guy.

As the evening wears on, it's more like watching a performance than having a conversation. His bellowing voice, theatrical hand-waving, and faux laughter is less savvy businessman and more hunky huckster. I'm deeply enthralled by the tales he is spinning, and the "Reclamation Project" is the furthest thing from my mind.

We discover that several years prior I had walked by his apartment in Manhattan every day for almost a year while I was taking my children to school. Five years later we meet in an obscure village in Spain. *What are the chances?*

Before we part for the evening, he offers to drive me to my next village along the Camino the following day. I am offended he doesn't understand my commitment to walking all 200 miles of the journey, and I suggest he ditch his car and join me on the path. He declines, but we hatch a plan to meet up in New York City a few weeks later, and I'm exhilarated by the thought of it.

I should've known when he leaves me a voicemail the next morning and unapologetically trips over my name, "Hi, Cathy or Catherine or whatever your name is …"

But daily texts along the Camino from him—his virtually whispered sweet nothings, often in Spanish—only add to the intrigue and anticipation of seeing him again.

Reality is merely an illusion,
albeit a very persistent one.

– ALBERT EINSTEIN

CHAPTER 14
SUMMER 2012

As I take off for the longest walking day of my fourteen-day trek, I'm both irritated with the mild hangover and elated by the reason for it. Having met Mr. Tall, Dark & Handsome the night before feels unthinkably serendipitous and, "What are the chances?" plays on auto-loop in my head.

After a few hours, I fall in step with an older gentleman from France. He wears a smart paisley scarf, far too feminine a look for most men I know, but it suits Jean perfectly. He tells me in his imperfect English that he walked part of the Camino ten years prior but had to leave suddenly because of a family health scare. He has daughters my age, and his warm, fatherly nature is making me wish I had this level of rapport with my own dad.

At one point, Jean and I discover we are lost and find it rather hilarious as the Camino is a well-worn path and very well marked with yellow arrows. Later we stumble upon a leather goods merchant in the middle of a field, and Jean surprises me with a scallop-shell necklace of brown leather on black string. He buys necklaces for his daughters as well.

I tell him about my divorce but don't mention the suddenly defunct "Reclamation Project" or the fairytale romance that's brewing. He relays the story of a couple who decided to end their long-term marriage and walked the Camino to mark the end of their path. In a twist, their experience along the way shifted their thinking, and they decided to stay married.

I burst into tears, and Jean, realizing how this has landed for me, tries to repair. He feels so bad for telling me the story that it's not long before I feel bad for his feeling bad. We have a chuckle and note the mystery of life. Who knows if they're even still together, he says. This is a charitable man.

After lunch Jean and I part as he's staying for the night in that village, and I have another several walking hours before I arrive at my destination of Villafranca del Bierzo. My feet are giving me trouble, and I realize I need to slow down if I want to make it.

Walking alone, I begin to notice the faint buzzing sound of massive power lines overhead. They are so high above me that I barely notice them. I begin imagining one of them snapping and falling down on me, alone as I was, with only the speck of a fellow pilgrim up ahead in the distance.

I tell the Camino the entire story of the unraveling of my marriage. As if talking to a friend, it's a single soliloquy, chronicling the places, people, and pathology as I understand them. I imagine it takes over two hours to tell, flowing out of me like lava, thick, red hot, and steady. Tears, yes. Theatrics, no.

Our story couldn't have ended any other way.

Before long I'm in the midst of the rolling hills of a massive vineyard. I keep noticing pink rosebushes at the end of each row and am intrigued. Assuming they're planted on a whim of the vineyard owner and for aesthetics, I later learn that like the canary in the coalmine, the roses provide early warning of mildew—a common grapevine killer.

In the midst of winter,
I found there was, within me,
an invincible summer.

– ALBERT CAMUS

CHAPTER 15
SUMMER 2012

I'm meeting Mr. Tall, Dark & Handsome for dinner at Jacques. I barrel through the door escaping the manic swirl of wind and a tornado warning in Manhattan and cut my foot on a piece of metal as I cross the threshold of the restaurant. I am swooning at the sight of him as we say hello again after a month and across a continent.

We sit in a blood-red leather corner booth in front of decorative, oversized champagne bottles. Dark wood-paneled walls line the white-clothed tables. So oblivious to the faceless patrons in the room and the storm ensuing outside, we are enchanted with one another—already intoxicated ahead of the bottle of red.

I fall into bed with him a few hours later, so lost in the story we'd surely tell our grandchildren one day.

I leave his apartment in the black of night, trying to dampen the clink-clink-clink of my heels on the cracked tile floor. Descending the stairs of his third-floor walk-up, I am silently chanting: *God, I hope he still respects me. God, I hope he still respects me. God, I hope he still respects me.*

By lunchtime, the magical love affair resumes and plays out over the next four days I am in the city. We spend almost the entire time together, day and night. We dash from this bar to that restaurant, from meeting this business associate to his fielding multiple texts and emails. It is all very rush-rush and at times hush-hush.

We go to a movie one afternoon, and while sitting in the theater, I have a fleeting thought: *Am I at a movie or in a movie?*

I should know it has little to do with him when it takes me nearly a year to recover from what couldn't have amounted to more than two weeks together spread out over several months. I know I can't blame him for what is nothing more than sport to him, but having met the way we did and discovering all the synchronicities, I simply cannot let go of the dream.

The romance-that-wasn't is extremely humbling and also revelatory. What is it about me that would settle for this kind of relationship so out of sync with my true desires? Why would I torture myself this way? *This is what the hungry do.*

And yet, how can I be anything but grateful to him? The universe plopped him down on my path, saving me from myself and my whackadoodle "Reclamation Project."

History doesn't repeat
itself, but it rhymes.

- MARK TWAIN

CHAPTER 16
FALL 2015

I t's parents weekend in Chapel Hill and Stuart and I decide to ride together to go see Julia. On the drive back home, he and I land on the topic of dating. At the time, we are both single, and he begins to enlighten me on some of the new dating websites. A prolific dater—something I'm still adjusting to, given the man I thought I knew—he encourages me to sign up for one of the newer sites that puts the woman in charge of reaching out.

Once home, I decide to get on Bumble.com, and within a few moments, I'm swiping through an array of men my age. Is it more bizarre that he suggests I try out Bumble or that he is one of the very first matches that pops up on my phone?

Or perhaps most bizarre is seeing him there and finding his photo and bio appealing, as if I hadn't known him since he was eighteen, seeing him for the first time at age fifty in a purple-striped, button-down shirt I didn't know he owned, exuding the same quiet confidence that pulled me in the first time.

Who is this man now? Would I choose him again?

"Finance jackass by day, Southern gentleman by night," it reads, and my chuckle turns teary before I swipe left.

While I have no interest in dating Stuart again, we are inextricably linked by a shared history spanning more than three decades. Who else knows he wants *Be Thou My Vision* played at his funeral? And preferably the Van Morrison version, though I suppose he'd settle for a group hymn rendition if secular music were frowned upon in the church like it was when we married in 1992.

He hasn't remarried and doesn't have a significant other in his life right now, so does that make me the default funeral planner? Are his daughters old enough at eighteen and twenty to plan it? Are his elderly parents expected (or expecting) to do it?

As I imagine it, the service would be overflowing with middle-aged prepsters driving dark SUVs and wearing expensive ties with tiny patterns of rabbits or horses or fish. There'd be a big turnout of his fraternity brothers in particular. They'd whisper "phi-phi" to each other or maybe just express it in glances—the secret code word whose meaning he'd never confess but that I took to mean something like, "For real, man, I speak the truth here."

Among the inner circle of brothers, there's a pack of them who descend upon Las Vegas each spring for March Madness (twenty-five-plus years running) and then travel to the Kentucky Derby six weeks later. The whole posse is on second wives—one on a third—but the man in the urn at this imagined funeral held to his word that he'd never marry again.

At the service our girls would be stoic. They look most like me but have their daddy's uncanny ability to curb emotion. They'd be the loveliest creatures there, floating through the afternoon with pluck and poise. Their mother wouldn't be faring nearly as well.

The girls were ten and twelve when we told them we were separating. The day of the scheduled announcement was a beautiful Friday afternoon in late spring. Earlier in the day, Stuart and I met at a nearby lake for a divorce ritual I'd planned for the two of us. I had a photo book of our life together, three days in the making, and was eager to share it with him.

From our first meeting at Myers Park High School in 1984 to the family vacation we'd recently taken with the girls to Key West, I was honoring the twenty-six years we'd spent in each other's orbit, and I was terribly proud of it. Ultimately for our girls, I wanted to show them all the happy years and prove we didn't marry the wrong person.

I walked away to give him privacy as he flipped through the book. He finished much sooner than I would have imagined.

"It looks like a funeral," he said.

The past is never dead.
It's not even past.

– WILLIAM FAULKNER

CHAPTER 17
SPRING 2014

Four years after we separate, I find myself writing a letter to Stuart inspired by listening to the online class called *Conscious Uncoupling* by Katherine Woodward Thomas. In an "amends and release letter," written over several days with the sole intention of delivering it to the person you are attempting to uncouple from, the author offers suggested language and topics to cover.

What this letter is *not* is one of those rants where you vomit all over the page and then burn it. While deeply satisfying and often incredibly therapeutic, that's not the model here.

My original impetus for taking the course is more curiosity than an actual need to uncouple. At the four-year mark, I'm feeling successfully uncoupled from him. But this "conscious uncoupling" thing—made famous by Gwyneth Paltrow and Chris Martin's split—sounds like healthy divorce-speak to me, and I'm intrigued.

Over the course of eight hours of passive listening and deep soul searching, I'm coming to understand that while we've lived separate lives and been "free agents" since the moment of separation, we're as psychologically and emotionally tied as ever. *His hooks are still in me. Dammit.*

The final product is a 1,700-word letter, parts of which appear here verbatim.

It starts with deep gratitude ...

> *I want to tell you how grateful I am for our life together and most especially for the eighteen years we were married. You took me places I could have never gone on my own. And I don't just mean two tours of duty in Manhattan. You were my rock from the beginning and helped me develop confidence in myself and trust in the universe. You swept me away to Ann Arbor and got me "off the tit" of my family, friends, and comfort zone. You showed me a great adventure in Chicago and made me ride bikes with a buzz. You took me back home to familiarity and warmth even with the tug of [an opportunity in Boston] calling. You let me quit work after the second miscarriage and went to grief counseling with me even while the grief wasn't yours. You gave me two beautiful children and the freedom to raise them with laser focus knowing it was my great joy.*

> *You taught me humility and discretion. You opened my eyes to the larger world by way of your job in NYC. You let me do anything and everything I wanted to do in the way of time with friends, educational opportunities, half-baked projects, rearranging rooms, and trading*

houses. You let me make decisions for our girls even when it was costly and you were opposed. You let me move us back and forth to the city twice and endured a four-year commute without ever complaining once even though it wasn't your idea or your preference. I could go on and on. I am so grateful for how you showed me love, and for the incredibly rich life we spent together.

Continues with a series of apologies …

I am terribly sorry for putting you in the situation of constantly having to prove your love and devotion to me. I am sorry for seldom recognizing the small things and for punishing you for not loving me the way I wanted to be loved. I am sorry that I didn't see that you loved me, and that your providing for me and our family was an incredible gift of love and devotion. I am sorry that nothing was ever enough for me. I am sorry I wasn't vulnerable enough with you, even while I was demanding it of you. I am sorry I resented your work and career and allowed myself to feel second to that. I am sorry that I didn't take you at your word that all you wanted was my happiness. I'm sorry for how I tried to turn you into the male version of me. I'm sorry I expected things of you that you weren't able to give. I am sorry for my contribution to the ending of our marriage.

And then a bid for forgiveness …

> *Please forgive me for all the ways that I failed*
> *to love you in the ways you desired to be loved,*
> *for things I may have said and done that have*
> *hurt you. Please forgive me for the ways I was*
> *unconscious, selfish, and thoughtless in our*
> *marriage. And I thank you from the bottom of*
> *my heart for all of the love and care that you have*
> *given me, both during our marriage and since.*

Lastly, the ritual of release …

> *With this letter I want to release us both from*
> *our old "agreements" (many unspoken): that*
> *we'd be married forever, that finding true love*
> *again is somehow disloyal to the love we once*
> *shared, that marrying again devalues the life we*
> *shared as a couple, that carving out a life with*
> *someone else negates the life we once shared as*
> *a family of four. I release the old ideas I've held*
> *about who I am, who you are, and who we were*
> *together. I release the expectation that you will*
> *always put me first, above any other woman. I*
> *release the expectation that you will always be*
> *there for me.*

Within a few hours of hitting the send button, I receive
from Stuart a brief and generous acknowledgment, part of
which read:

> *This whole thing resonates. We did the best*
> *we could knowing what we knew. Don't beat*

yourself up about it for sure. I have felt everything
you have.

As is our norm, his response compared to mine comes in at a ratio of approximately 1:35. Brevity aside, I am incredibly grateful for his empathic response.

There are years
that ask questions
and years that answer.

– ZORA NEALE HURSTON

CHAPTER 18
2010—2015

From the moment we separate, I am eager to date and feel perfectly within my right to do so, and I know Stuart feels the same way. I know he is dating, even though we share an unarticulated "don't ask/don't tell" rule. And while I don't want to hear about it or even think about it, I don't begrudge him the same freedom and happiness that I seek.

I'm committed to the process, always game to be set up by friends and, despite intermittent vacations, a frequent flier on multiple dating websites. The "possibilitarian" in me is hungry for real connection, so I accept *a lot* of dates. And while I meet a few exceptionally interesting people, I suffer through drinks and dinner with plenty of men with whom I have very little in common.

At dinner one night I say something (apparently) snarky to my date, and he slams his water glass on the table so forcefully that it shatters. I'm dumbstruck but proceed to tolerate our dinner in some twisted attempt to help him save face when what I really want to do is suggest he register for anger management classes. His "look what you made me do" is met with a raised brow and an internal fantasy of excusing myself and crawling out the bathroom window. *Look what you're making me do.*

Another time I meet a guy for beers, and it's obvious he's been drinking. Heavily. He's slurring his words and asking me the same questions repeatedly. We have a common friend, and I don't want to seem prudish, so I keep up the charade that we're having a good time together. He's a sweet drunk, but I'm surprised by how unseemly being hammered looks even on the most handsome of faces.

Quirks and proclivities collide the night I meet the guy who orders a glass of milk for himself. At the bar. And with no explanation. *How did I misread this one so spectacularly? And is forty-five minutes long enough to count as a date?*

And then there's the one whose ego is the third member at our brunch table for two. As he's going on and on about his professional success—the type of person who's awfully happy with how he's turned out—he tells me of his interest in me as if I've passed some sort of test. That I have no intention of going out on a second date with him and am politely enduring the meal hasn't occurred to him. When I run into him a few years later he introduces me to his friend as "the one who wouldn't go out on a second date with me."

You're no Stuart Friou is the bubble language that often floats over my head. Never spoken and seldom even consciously thought, it's a high hurdle each of my dating partners has to clear. I'm looking for a mix of intelligence, sophistication, self-confidence, and sure-footedness that proves much harder to find than I thought it would be—to say nothing of wanting to feel physical attraction too.

I'm starting to wonder if my desire to fire on all cylinders with a person is too much to ask, and I'm growing weary.

It's better to be wrong
than to be vague.

– FREEMAN DYSON

CHAPTER 19
SUMMER 2014

"Can you meet for beers? I need you to talk me off the ledge," I bang out quickly on text.

I have just learned that Stuart has taken his girlfriend along on a beach trip with our kids, and I'm texting my friend (and former pseudo-boyfriend) for a lifeline. With my heart in my throat as I type, I am equal parts furious and heartbroken. He meets me an hour later.

I feel better almost immediately, though I can't decide if it's his calming presence or the pint of Stella I'm downing. Sometime that afternoon as we're gabbing nonstop, I catch a glimpse of him that takes me by surprise. Cocking my head I think to myself, *Hmm, I wouldn't mind kissing you again.*

I am so desperately craving normal. If I have to go out on one more Match.com date with one more ill-matched suitor, I am going to self-destruct. Four years out and still single will do that to a girl. Surely he knows how depleted I am by it all.

We originally met on eharmony.com a few years prior. He was one of only two dates from my short time on that dating site, and I'd been the one to reach out to him. I think it was the beach photo that did it—sweet, boyish, tanned face—clearly cropped. I imagine his smiling ex-wife was on his left in the original photo.

We had one of the best first dates I'd ever had, and he said the same. He was slightly overdressed—what with that pocket square and all—but it was an incredibly comfortable and festive evening. The several dates that followed were enjoyable, but ultimately it felt more like friendship to me. Plus, he didn't kiss me like he meant it.

He took the news that I didn't want to continue dating back then pretty well, and a great friendship ensued. We often compare notes and exchange eye rolls about some of the nutty people we meet along the way. He is supremely dependable, always up for grabbing a drink and dissecting the rare air of midlife dating.

A few weeks after he talks me off the ledge, he tells me he senses there is something between us worth exploring, something worth fighting for, and asks me to trust him. He wants us to give it another go, and I'm pleasantly surprised by his confession. His vulnerability that day is incredibly attractive to me.

And then he kisses me like he means it.

Accessible, responsive, and engaged, he is boyfriend extraordinaire from that moment forward. We date for a little over a year, and I introduce him to my children and my parents—a first on both counts. We hop from one adventure to another and privately joke that it must suck not to be us in the way only those drunk on their own love do.

It feels like my first full-fledged relationship because he's all in from the start. He is not torn, and this is not sport. He is certain about us as a couple and clear that he wants a future together. I admire this in him and long to feel it too.

But I'm riddled with ambivalence, and all the gold in his heart can't outshine that ugly reality.

I want him to be my person. He should be my person. It's past time to have met my person. He's a loving, generous, first-class person. He's not my person.

There is no truth, only
points of view.

– EDITH SITWELL

CHAPTER 20
2006–2015

My children have moved so many times we sometimes joke that the most consistent address they've known is that of their grandparents. Both girls have been dropping by the house I grew up in since they were in utero. But the girls' primary home base for the last ten years is an unassuming beach house with a peekaboo view of the ocean on the Isle of Palms in South Carolina.

There's a lemon tree on the side of the house with dreadfully tart fruit and two-inch thorns and an overgrown live oak in the backyard. The burly oak lovingly nestles the house, wrapping its curly branches around the second-floor screened porch. A Carolina-blue golf cart is a driveway fixture, and a navy blue Palmetto State flag hangs off the front porch.

A handful of years after we bought the beach house, we divorce but continue to co-own the house and enjoy it separately. While I sometimes take the kids or a friend, typically I go to the beach house alone. And my first stop is always the back porch to say hello to my oak tree.

The screened porch feels like a tree house to me, and I spend a lot of time reading and reflecting under the canopy of that tree. I read somewhere that trees absorb grief, and whether true or not, I count that particular live oak as a part of my healing process.

When the tree begins to look unruly, I decide it is time for another trim. The mangled limbs from a botched trim several years before left me heartsick, so this time I decide to invest in an arborist.

After a most artful pruning, a truly exquisite tree emerges. A sunset view I never knew we had reveals itself hours later. The newly restored tree seems to be reveling in its majesty, no longer collapsing under its own weight.

Five years after the divorce, I choose to sell my half of the house to Stuart. It seems long enough to still co-own the family beach house. More soul imperative than business decision, I sense it's time for me to let go and allow space for something new to take root.

One winter when I'm in town renting my own place, I ride my bike by the house, knowing it's unoccupied. Assuming I'd be a welcome interloper, I make my way through the unhinged gate and pass the lemon tree bursting with as much yellow as I've ever seen. Approaching the back yard to visit my tree, I realize quickly by the lack of canopy that it's been trimmed. I feel a pit in my stomach as my eyes begin to well. Soon I'm doubled over, sobbing.

My tree is disfigured and sad looking, even brown in some places, and not the lush, vibrant monster I'd seen in

Rock Paper Scissors

summers past. I'm heartbroken at the sight of it and surprised by my dramatic reaction.

I text Stuart and say I want to retrieve a board game that's meaningful to me. It's partially true, but what I really want is a closer look at that tree from inside the porch as I always used to see it. *Maybe it's not that bad.*

> I'm at the beach. Do you mind if I go in the house and get a board game called *Ticket to Ride?* I bought it several years ago and would like it back. Or if you prefer, you can fetch it for me next time you're here.

Sure. I cleaned all that out.
May have given to charity

> Well bummer. That was a $50 game. All the other ones appear to still be there. Maybe I got it from you before (?)

Gave plenty of them away

> Who trimmed the tree? Clearly not the arborist I hired before.

Hank. Tree be fine come spring

> I remember it full this summer when Julia had me over. Way past needing a trim for sure.

Scenes from a Charmed Divorce

It looks mangled and sad but
will fill in some yes. I cried
when I saw it. (Literally)

————  four hours later  ————

I assume you want to renew
AAA on the family plan

It's terribly amusing how many
different climates of feeling
one can go through in a day.

– ANNE MORROW LINDBERGH

CHAPTER 21
SUMMER 2017

I frame my very first photo of me with another man. My boyfriend and I have been together for more than a year, and it's a picture of us from a backyard band party in the fall. The photo of us sits on my desk just beyond the view of my laptop screen. Even after it sits there for several months, I'm still sometimes surprised to see not-my-husband guy and me. It's always a nanosecond of *Oh yeah, this is my new life and my new love.*

It's strange to hold two loves at the same time. There is my current love, someone I can no longer imagine my life without. And then there is Stuart, my former love and life partner—the one I assumed would be my forever.

I look at my boyfriend's profile as he drives us to dinner, and I catch myself staring at him, really drinking him in. *Those are the sideburns of my beloved. I'll be seeing and loving that face for the next fifty years.* Gratitude and joy envelop me. Suddenly, the six-year wait to find my person seems reasonable.

And I feel vulnerable. I fell in love with him early and unequivocally and have stronger feelings for him than any other person since my marriage ended. I also feel tentative at times and wonder if some of the old "agreements" with Stuart are still lurking about—that finding true love again is somehow disloyal to the love we once shared, that marrying again devalues the life we shared as a couple, that carving out a life with someone else negates the life we once shared as a family of four.

I joke that divorce is the gift that keeps on giving. The shared history, the shared children, the container that is marriage and family is a narrative that's sometimes hard to outrun.

We must be willing to
let go of the life we've
planned, so as to have the
life that is waiting for us.

- JOSEPH CAMPBELL

CHAPTER 22
SUMMER 2017

As we're readying our youngest to go off to college and moving our older daughter into her first apartment, the ghosts that await me in Stuart's house take me by surprise.

Fetching something for one of our kids, I see pieces of furniture I forgot we had. There's the club chair from one of our early houses, since reupholstered, twice (and in desperate need of a third recovering). There's the chair that our first baby, a mischievous beagle, used to curl up on and sleep at the back of Stuart's neck while Stuart watched *SportsCenter*.

I spy a New Yorker cartoon, yellowed and curled, taped to the wall near Stuart's desk. An urban couple is sitting on their terrace with one lamenting, "It's not that I love New York. It's just that I hate everyplace else."

I chuckle, and it reminds me of the cartoon I laminated a few houses back when we were still together. A couple is rocking on their porch in a bucolic New England town, and one of them sighs, "I miss hating the city."

Next, I turn and see the mahogany rice bed Stuart's parents gave us as a wedding gift twenty-five years ago. Over time it was replaced and moved to the guest room, but he took it as his own when he moved out. I gaze at it, speculating how many women have been there and wonder if he's been in love with any of them. I wonder if there are far more or far fewer than I might think, and I begin to imagine what he'd make of my "number."

I come to Claire's room, and a pang hits. Guilt? Regret? Melancholy? Pride that I was always able to create a series of comfortable cocoons for our disjointed family?

I know a woman who left a month's worth of dinners in the freezer for her ex-husband. Perhaps Stuart wouldn't be as skinny had I done that, though meal-making was never my love language. But give me an empty dwelling, and with great gusto I can whip up a five-star living experience in a New York minute.

A bird doesn't sing because
it has an answer, it sings
because it has a song.

– MAYA ANGELOU

CHAPTER 23
LATE SUMMER 2017

Claire and I fly to New York City sooner than planned to leave us plenty of time to do the final push for dorm shopping and the ability to play tourist when Julia joins the rest of the family in the city.

Staying in my friend Jennifer's apartment while she was away is convenient being just a few stoops down from Stuart's apartment. And her beautiful rooftop has a 270-degree view of Manhattan, including an unmarred view of the apartment we'd moved into as a family exactly ten years prior.

Stuart joins me for a glass of wine on the rooftop. He and I are on one couch, and Claire sits on the other. She takes a photo of the two of us, and I see later on her Facebook page a doctored photo with crown stickers on us, one that says mother and one that says father. Always a compliment when we happen to make the well-curated social media platforms of our children, this post feels particularly heartwarming.

It's not uncommon for Stuart and me to share a glass of wine. We have spent many evenings together over the last seven years. Almost all of them have been with the kids, but there was the occasional post-back-to-school-night drink peppering the years since we'd parted.

I insisted he hang out with me after we dropped Julia at college two years prior. I booked him weeks in advance so I wouldn't be alone that first night. We had wine on his porch and later ordered Indian food. It was as comfortable as anything we used to do while married.

Is it weird for our girls that their parents are so friendly? They've never known us any other way, married or divorced, but clearly we aren't the norm. Is it confusing? Has it been, in the words of our marriage and family therapist, "different enough"? We entrusted this man with the health and well being of our marriage, our divorce, and our family. His main concern, given our supreme civility, was that things wouldn't be different enough for the kids to understand we'd divorced.

It occurs to me now—has it been different enough for us?

On the fourth night in a row of having a drink on the rooftop before heading out to dinner, I share a photo book with the three of them. It's a smattering of photos of the girls chronicling their years as city kids. The first photos are of Claire still in her stroller.

The only family shot in the bunch I'm sharing is the one taken on Claire's second birthday. A broad view of lower Manhattan is the backdrop for our boat ride on the Staten Island ferry. The Twin Towers are shining in the distance well above the skyline. Grinning and giddy, we'd been living in the city less than a week when the photo was taken. Two weeks later the towers fell.

The photo book doesn't seem as poignant to the girls as I thought it might be. *Look how far you've come, people!* seems to be secondary to the excitement of where we are as a family right now and the dinner we're headed to downtown to celebrate Claire's eighteenth birthday.

"Mom's crying again," says Claire in a cab on our way home from dinner.

"You never did all this for me. So typical," laments Julia.

"I'm not crying," I lie.

The following day finds the four of us perched on a bench in the middle of Broadway. We've just finished moving Claire into her dorm and are catching flights out soon. We eat lunch in the median, life and traffic bustling all around us.

An unseasonably cool day in late August, on an unlikely set of empty benches, we devour burgers and fries from a wildly popular place Claire can see from her dorm window on 116th Street. We flag a student to take our photo, and a few minutes later we say goodbye to Claire on the corner.

Later that afternoon I'll be flying to Charleston for a glorious buffer week at the beach with my boyfriend. I'll jump into his arms on the curb of arriving flights and nestle not only into his neck but also our new life together—an emotionally generous, emerging life that feels as essential as the one I've just left behind. And equally incalculable.

But for now I'm feeling both sentimental and serene. The weekend has exceeded my expectations on so many levels. Principally, it's been a festive closing ceremony for parenthood, a four-day toast to a job well done. Despite the divorce and now living in four separate places, we are as deeply connected and united a family as ever.

When Stuart and I first separated, it felt like an intentional shattering of something wondrous and whole—something that didn't have to happen but did happen.

Not long after, I took a teacup from our fine china pattern and smashed it into oblivion on the driveway. It was mildly cathartic, but I'm grateful our story didn't end there. We're more like *kintsugi*, the centuries-old Japanese art of mending broken pottery with a golden lacquer. Our family's history of breaks and repairs is highlighted instead of hidden, and we have transformed it into our own kind of beautiful.

Out beyond ideas of
wrongdoing and rightdoing,
there is a field. I'll meet you there.

– RUMI

ACKNOWLEDGMENTS

It takes all manner of help, both visible and invisible, to write a book.

I'm deeply appreciative of my writing teachers and for the professional editing I've received from Maureen Ryan Griffin, Nancy Aronie, Joanne Fedler, Melisa Graham, Kristin Sherman, and Kim Wright.

To my beta readers, all of whom are dear friends and some of whom are writers themselves—Kelley Snyder, Libby Wagner, Jennifer Flanders, Amy Ormond, Hannelore Bragg, Jessie Thompson, and especially Kathie Collins—thank you all for the soul read. You have my everlasting gratitude.

To Stuart, my good sport of an ex-husband, who read (and blessed) my final draft, thank you for navigating and embracing the co-parenting thing with me.

And to my daughters, Julia and Claire, being your mother has always been my great joy. You enrich my life in ways you will never understand until you are mothers yourselves. I love you two to the moon and back, as ever.

ABOUT THE AUTHOR

Cathia Friou (Cathy-uh Free-oh) is a healthy-divorce advocate and co-parenting specialist. Formally trained as a leadership coach and mediator, she is an ardent devotee of self-awareness, courageous conversations, and conflict transformation. She is endlessly fascinated with people, relationships, and systems, and believes, as Socrates, that the unexamined life is not worth living. Please visit www.cathiafriou.com.

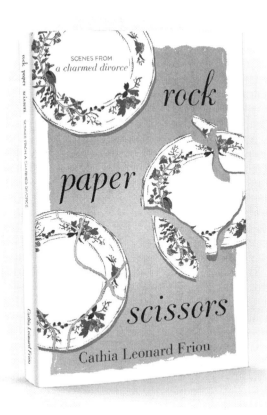

*If you know someone who is
contemplating divorce or smack
dab in the middle of it, please
share a copy of this book.*

Made in the USA
Lexington, KY
17 May 2018